It's STILL ALIVE!

Magical Animals That Regrow Parts

by Nikki Potts

CAPSTONE PRESS
a capstone imprint

A+ books

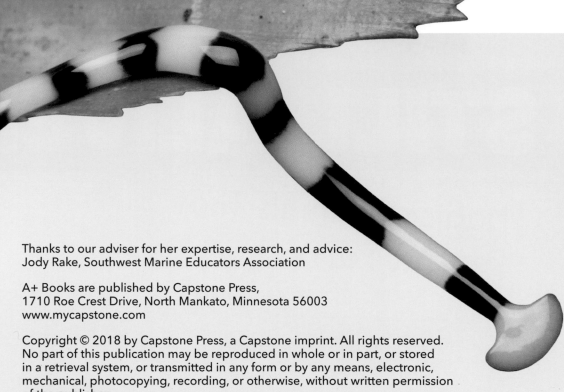

Thanks to our adviser for her expertise, research, and advice:
Jody Rake, Southwest Marine Educators Association

A+ Books are published by Capstone Press,
1710 Roe Crest Drive, North Mankato, Minnesota 56003
www.mycapstone.com

Library of Congress Cataloging-in-Publication Data
Library of Congress Cataloging-in-Publication Data is available on the Library of
Congress website.

ISBN: 978-1-5157-9463-9 (library hardover) —
978-1-5157-9467-7 (paperback) – 978-1-5157-9471-4 (ebook)

Summary: A look at animals that regenerate body parts

Editorial Credits
Jaclyn Jaycox, editor; Ashlee Suker, designer; Tracy Cummins, media researcher;
Tori Abraham, production specialist

Photo Credits
Alamy: Shay Levy, 16; iStockphoto: somethingway, 28, wblom, 11; Minden
Pictures: Alex Mustard, 15, Sue Daly, 9; Newscom: W. Layer/picture alliance/
blickwinkel, 17; Science Source: Dr. Keith Wheeler, 21, Eye of Science, 27, James
H. Robinson, 13, Tom McHugh, 22; Shutterstock: 3Dstock, 26, Adam Kel, 8,
Cigdem Sean Cooper, 29, Decha Thapanya, 4-5, dossyl, Cover Back, 12, Ethan
Daniels, 19, George P Gross, 14, Kazakov Maksim, 24, kurt_G Stock, Cover, Matt
Jeppson, 23, Najmie Naharuddin, 2, 20, reptiles4all, 1, Rich Carey, 18, Robert F
Apple, 10, Sergio Gutierrez Getino, 6, topimages, 25, Victor Saul, 7

Note to Parents, Teachers, and Librarians
This Magical Animals book uses full color photographs and a nonfiction format to
introduce the concept of regeneration. *It's Still Alive!* is designed to be read aloud
to a pre-reader or to be read independently by an early reader. Photographs
help listeners and early readers understand the text and concepts discussed. The
book encourages further learning by including the following sections: Table of
Contents, Glossary, Read More, Internet Sites, Critical Thinking Questions, and
Index. Early readers may need assistance using these features.

Printed and bound in the United States of America.
010851S18

TABLE OF CONTENTS

Mexican Axolotl 6

Sea Star 8

Spider 10

Anole Lizard 12

Conch 15

African Spiny Mouse 16

Sea Cucumber 19

Flatworm 20

Gecko 23

Zebrafish 25

Water Bear 26

Moon Jellyfish 28

Glossary 30

Read More 31

Internet Sites 31

Critical Thinking Questions 32

Index 32

Look! That spider is missing a leg! But don't worry, it will grow back. Some animals can regrow their limbs, organs, and skin. This is called regeneration. Many animals lose body parts while escaping from predators. A lost limb distracts the predator and gives the animal a chance to get away.

MEXICAN AXOLOTL

Mexican axolotls are found in waters near Mexico City. Unlike many amphibians, axolotls keep their gills into adulthood. Axolotls can be up to 12 inches (30 centimeters) long. Most axolotls live for up to 15 years. They are able to regenerate many body parts. Limbs, jaws, tails, skin, and spinal cords can all be regrown.

Axolotls can be black, brown, white, or albino. Mexican axolotls are an endangered species.

SEA STAR

Sea stars are also known as starfish. But they are not fish. Sea stars live in deep or shallow ocean water. There are 2,000 species of sea stars. The largest can weigh nearly 11 pounds (5 kilograms). Most sea stars have five arms. But some species have up to 40 arms! A sea star's arms often contain its most important organs. Many species can regrow arms. Some sea stars can regrow a whole new body from just part of one arm.

SPIDER

Spiders are found on every continent except Antarctica. Plenty of predators hunt for spiders. A predator might damage a spider's leg by biting it. The spider then often detaches its leg for defense. This is called autotomy. Losing the leg may save the spider's life. The leg will grow back in time.

missing legs

:: FUN FACT ::

Spiders aren't considered insects. They are arachnids.
Insects have six legs and three body sections.
Arachnids have only two body sections and eight legs.

ANOLE LIZARD

Anole lizards are also masters of autotomy. This lizard contracts muscles in order to cut off its tail. The detached tail distracts predators. Later, a new tail grows in its place. The new tail is made of cartilage instead of bones. Anole lizards are found throughout the southern United States. Most do not live more than three years in the wild.

13

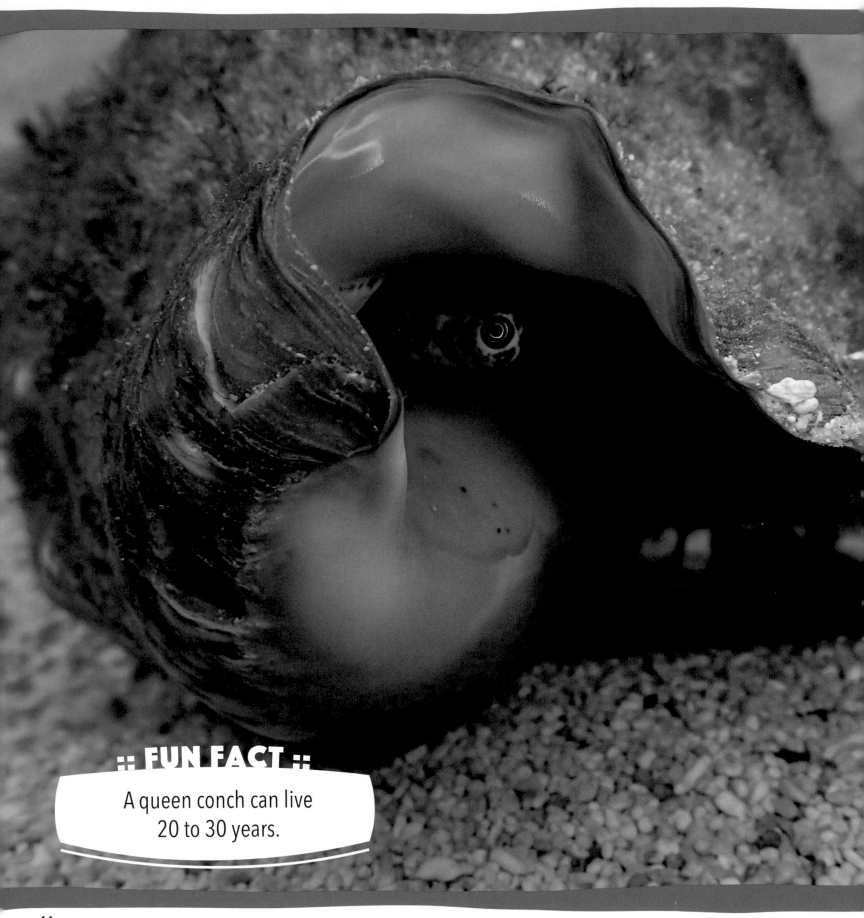

A queen conch can live
20 to 30 years.

CONCH

Conchs are saltwater snails. A conch has a spiral shell with short spikes sticking out. An adult's shell can be 6 to 12 inches (15 to 30 cm) long. A conch has excellent vision. This snail is able to pull its eyes into its shell. But a fast predator can bite off the snail's eyes. A conch can fully regrow its eyes in just two weeks!

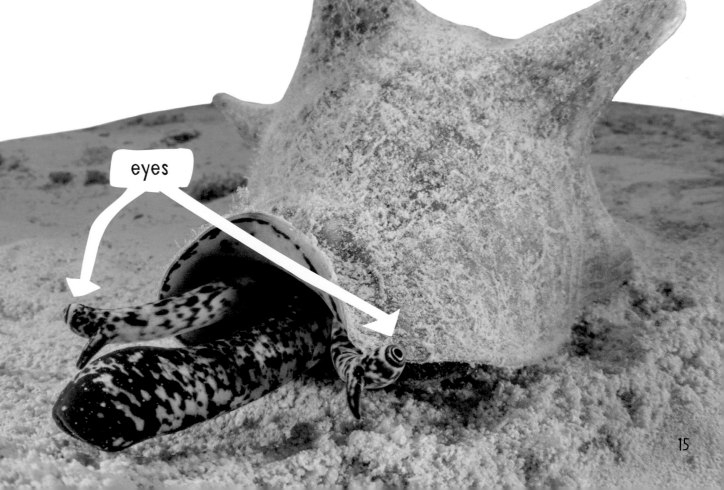

eyes

AFRICAN SPINY MOUSE

The African spiny mouse has skin that can be easily torn. The mouse may lose its skin after a predator attack. This helps the mouse escape. The African spiny mouse can regenerate its skin right after an injury. This is called skin autotomy. It is the first mammal discovered to have this ability.

SEA CUCUMBER

There are more than 1,250 known species of sea cucumbers. They are found near the ocean floor. Sea cucumbers can shoot sticky threads and internal organs at their predators. This confuses the predator so the sea cucumber can get away. Its missing organs regrow quickly. Sea cucumbers live for five to 10 years.

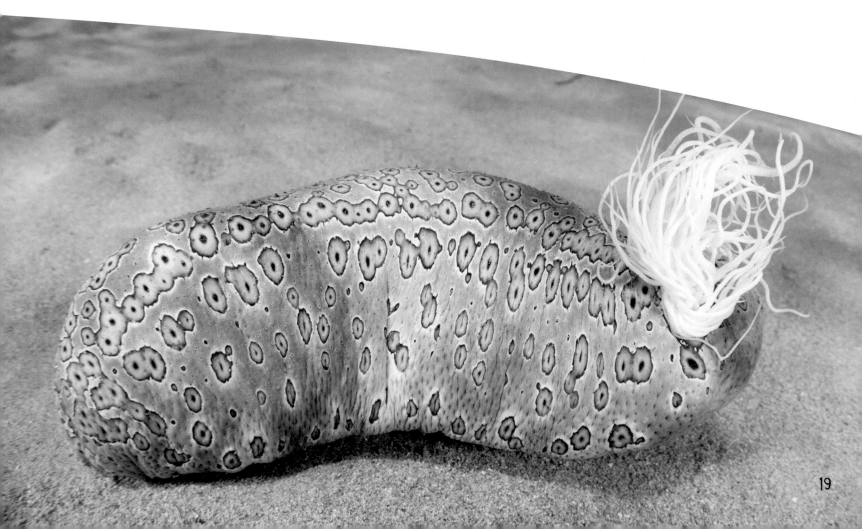

FLATWORM

Flatworms are found in places with moist land. They can be as small as 0.04 inches (0.1 cm). But some can grow to 24 inches (61 cm)! There are more than 20,000 flatworm species. A flatworm can lose most of its body and regrow from just a small piece. A flatworm is different than most other worms. Its tail can regrow a head. And its head can regrow a tail!

GECKO

Geckos use their tails for balance when climbing trees. Some species also use their tails for camouflage. They can blend in with tree bark. Gecko tails have weak points in them. At these weak spots, the tail can break off. The fallen tail continues to move. It distracts predators so the gecko has time to escape! One, sometimes two, tails grow back in its place.

:: FUN FACT ::

Geckos are found all around the world, except in Antarctica. They can live in forests, deserts, and mountainous areas.

ZEBRAFISH

Zebrafish are freshwater fish originally from India. A zebrafish has two heart chambers. It can regrow its heart muscle. Damaged muscle returns to nearly its original size and shape. A zebrafish can also regrow other body parts. It regenerates bones, blood vessels, and nerves in its fins.

WATER BEAR

Tiny water bears live in water in almost every habitat on Earth. A water bear can live in very hot or very cold weather. It can survive in temperatures as low as minus 328 degrees Fahrenheit (minus 200 degrees Celsius). To survive, it goes into a deathlike state. It can go without food or water for more than 30 years! When put back into water, a water bear comes back to life—even years later.

:: **FUN FACT** ::
Water bears are also known as tardigrades.

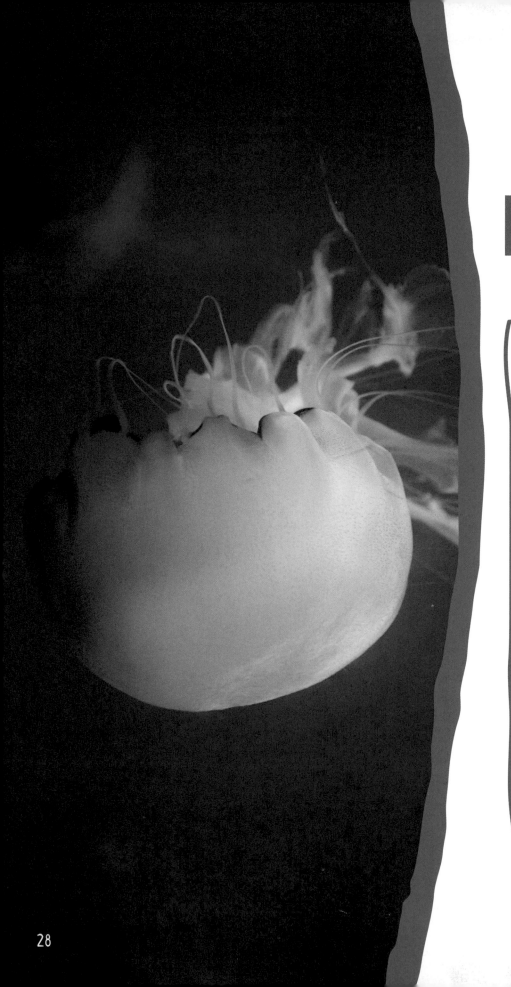

MOON JELLYFISH

Moon jellyfish are found in warm, open ocean waters. They eat small plankton, fish eggs, and other small jellies. A moon jellyfish has hair-like parts called cilia. Sometimes a predator takes a bite out of the cilia. The moon jellyfish doesn't regenerate body parts like most jellies. Instead, a moon jellyfish rearranges the remaining cilia to fill in the space.

:: FUN FACT ::

A moon jellyfish's color depends on what it eats. A pink or purple jellyfish likely eats crustaceans. An orange jellyfish may be eating brine shrimp.

GLOSSARY

AMPHIBIAN—an animal that lives in the water when it is young and on land as an adult; some amphibians, such as frogs, can live both in the water and on land as adults

AUTOTOMY—the ability of some animals to safely shed a damaged or trapped body part

BARK—hard covering of a tree

BLOOD VESSEL—a narrow tube that carries blood through the body

CAMOUFLAGE—a pattern or color on an animal's skin that helps it blend in with the things around it

CARTILAGE—the strong, bendable material that forms some body parts on humans and animals

CONTRACT—to tighten and become shorter

DETACH—to separate one thing from another

LIMB—a part of the body used in moving or grasping; arms and legs are limbs

MAMMAL—a warm-blooded animal that breathes air; mammals have hair or fur

NERVE—a thin fiber that carries messages between the brain and other parts of the body

ORGAN—a body part that does a certain job

PLANKTON—tiny plants and animals that drift in the sea

REGENERATE—to make new

SPECIES—a group of animals with similar features

SURVIVE—to stay alive

Read MORE

Gibbs, Maddie. *Sea Stars*. Fun Fish. New York: PowerKids Press, 2014.

Rake, Jody S., *Sea Cucumbers*. Faceless, Spineless, and Brainless Ocean Animals. North Mankato, Minn.: Capstone Press, 2017.

Rustad, Martha E. H., *Stunning Spiders*. Bugs Are Beautiful! North Mankato, Minn.: Capstone Press, 2017.

Internet SITES

Use FactHound to find Internet sites related to this book.

Visit www.facthound.com

Just type in 9781515794639 and go.

Super-cool stuff! Check out projects, games and lots more at **www.capstonekids.com**

Critical Thinking QUESTIONS

1. Which body part can a conch regrow?

2. The African spiny mouse is the first mammal discovered to have the ability to regrow its skin. What is a mammal? Hint: Use your glossary for help!

3. Which animal in this book is your favorite? Why?

::INDEX::

amphibians, 6

autotomy, 10, 12, 16

bones, 12, 25

colors, 7, 29

lifespan, 6, 12, 14, 19

limbs, 4, 6, 8

mammals, 16

oceans, 8, 19, 28

organs, 4, 8, 19

predators, 4, 10, 12, 15, 16, 19, 23, 28

size, 6, 8, 15, 20, 25, 26

skin, 4, 6, 16

species, 8, 19, 20, 23

tails, 6, 12, 20, 23